The Gift They Never Knew They Needed
By: Matthew Petchinsky

Introduction: The Power of Unexpected Gifts: Why the Right Gift Matters More Than You Think

Imagine a moment when you've given someone a gift—a truly thoughtful one. Maybe it was a book that spoke to their hidden passion, a handmade token of love, or an experience they'd always dreamed of but never pursued. Their eyes lit up, their voice caught in their throat, and the gratitude they expressed wasn't just polite—it was real. That moment, fleeting as it was, carried a profound truth: the right gift isn't just a transaction; it's an emotional bridge, a way of saying, "I see you."

This book is not about materialism or the superficial exchange of items. Instead, it delves into the psychology and power of gifting. It explores how the act of giving, when done thoughtfully, becomes a profound expression of connection, love, and understanding. Gifts, when chosen well, have the ability to transcend words, repair strained relationships, and even create memories that linger long after the item itself fades into history.

The Psychology of Gifting

Why do we give gifts? From ancient times to modern days, the act of giving has been woven into the fabric of human culture. Anthropologists suggest that gifting originated as a means of building alliances, signaling status, and strengthening community bonds. Today, the motivations behind gifting remain complex and multifaceted. We give to express love, show appreciation, celebrate milestones, or simply bring joy to someone else. But at its core, the act of gifting taps into a primal need: the desire to connect.

Research has shown that giving a thoughtful gift lights up the same areas of the brain associated with happiness and reward. In fact, the giver often derives as much joy—if not more—than the recipient. This phenomenon, sometimes referred to as the "giver's glow," highlights the inherent reward in acts of generosity. But here's the catch: not all gifts elicit this reaction.

The wrong gift, even if expensive, can feel hollow or impersonal. It risks creating a sense of obligation or disappointment, leaving the recipient feeling unseen. Conversely, the *right* gift—a thoughtful, unexpected, and meaningful one—can spark joy, deepen relationships, and create a ripple effect of positivity. This book is about teaching you how to find and give *that* kind of gift.

Why This Book Will Change Your Perspective on Giving

For too long, gifting has been approached as a chore, a checkbox to tick during birthdays, holidays, or special occasions. Many people rush through stores or browse online, searching for something—*anything*—that feels "good enough." The result? Generic, uninspired gifts that often miss the mark.

This book offers a different approach. It's not about spending more money or following trends; it's about shifting your mindset. Through a blend of psychology, creativity, and practical advice, this book will transform the way you think about gifts, making the act of giving a joyful and fulfilling experience for both you and the recipient.

In the chapters ahead, you'll discover:

- The secrets to creating emotional resonance through gifts.
- How to break free from traditional norms and redefine what makes a "perfect" gift.
- Practical techniques for crafting or choosing gifts that feel deeply personal and memorable.
- The art of presenting and delivering gifts in a way that maximizes their impact.

Why the Unexpected Matters

Unexpected gifts hold a special kind of magic. They catch the recipient off guard, breaking the monotony of their day and making them feel uniquely valued. This book will teach you how to harness the element of surprise—not as a gimmick, but as a powerful tool to amplify the emotional impact of your gift. Whether it's a small, heartfelt gesture or a grand, life-changing present, the unexpected has the power to create lasting memories.

A World in Need of Connection

In an increasingly digital and disconnected world, the art of gifting has the potential to rebuild bridges. A thoughtful gift is more than just an item; it's a tangible representation of love, care, and understanding. It says, "I see you. I know you. I value you." This message is universal, transcending cultural and linguistic barriers.

As you turn these pages, prepare to embark on a journey that will revolutionize how you approach gift-giving. You'll not only learn practical skills but also cultivate a deeper appreciation for the emotional and psychological power of this timeless tradition. By the time you finish this book, you'll be equipped to give the kinds of gifts that people never forget—the ones that spark joy, deepen connections, and make the world a little brighter.

So, let's begin. Let's discover the gift they never knew they needed.

Chapter 1: The Art of Surprise

The best gifts are those that evoke genuine emotion, and at the heart of every great gift lies an element of surprise. Surprise isn't just about giving something unexpected—it's about creating a moment of wonder that lingers long after the gift is unwrapped. It's about breaking the routine of predictability and injecting a spark of delight into someone's day. In this chapter, we'll explore the psychology of surprise, why it's so impactful, and how to use it effectively in your gifting.

The Science of Surprise: Why It Matters

Surprise is a powerful psychological tool. When we experience something unexpected, our brains release dopamine, the chemical associated with pleasure, learning, and memory. This neurological reaction explains why surprises often feel more intense and memorable than planned events.

Surprises also disrupt our brain's predictive patterns. Humans are creatures of habit, and our brains are constantly making predictions about what will happen next. When something defies those expectations—like receiving a completely unforeseen gift—it forces our minds to pause and focus on the moment. This heightened attention amplifies the emotional impact of the experience.

Moreover, surprise triggers an emotional response that strengthens bonds. It signals thoughtfulness and effort, which can make the recipient feel deeply valued. In gifting, surprise isn't about being flashy or extravagant; it's about being intentional and meaningful.

How to Master the Art of Surprise in Gifting

1. **Know Your Recipient**
   Surprise only works when it aligns with the recipient's personality, preferences, and interests. A surprise gift that feels disconnected or irrelevant can fall flat—or worse, feel insincere. Start by observing and listening. Pay attention to their hobbies, passions, and even casual comments about things they like or wish they had. The more you understand their world, the easier it will be to surprise them in a way that resonates.
2. **Think Beyond the Obvious**
   The best surprises are those that feel personal and thoughtful. Instead of focusing on traditional gift categories like clothing or gadgets, consider experiences, handmade items, or symbolic gifts. For example, if someone loves stargazing, a surprise could be a custom star map of the night sky on a significant date in their life.
3. **Timing Is Everything**
   The timing of your surprise can enhance its impact. While birthdays and holidays are obvious occasions, surprising someone "just because" can feel even more special. Imagine giving a gift on a random Tuesday, simply because you wanted to brighten their day. The unexpectedness of the timing itself adds an extra layer of delight.
4. **Create a Story Around the Gift**
   A gift with a story is more impactful than one without context. Share why you chose it, how you found it, or what inspired you. For instance, if you're giving someone a vintage book, tell them how you stumbled upon it in a dusty little

shop that reminded you of them. The story adds depth and emotional significance to the gift.

5. **Use Mystery and Anticipation**

    Building anticipation can heighten the surprise. You might give small hints leading up to the gift or wrap it in an unconventional way that piques curiosity. For example, instead of simply handing over a wrapped box, you could create a scavenger hunt that leads them to the gift. The journey becomes part of the experience.

6. **Don't Underestimate Small Gestures**

    Not all surprises need to be grand or expensive. A handwritten note tucked into their bag, a favorite snack left on their desk, or a playlist curated just for them can carry as much emotional weight as a larger gift. These small, unexpected gestures can make someone feel seen and appreciated.

Crafting Emotional Moments That Last a Lifetime

While the surprise itself is impactful, the emotions it evokes are what truly make it memorable. Here are some ways to ensure your gift creates a lasting emotional impression:

1. **Tailor the Gift to a Shared Memory**
   Gifts that reference a shared experience or inside joke create an immediate emotional connection. For example, if you and a friend once joked about taking a pottery class together, surprising them with a pottery kit shows not only thoughtfulness but also a deep understanding of your bond.

2. **Appeal to the Senses**
   Engaging the senses can make a gift more immersive and memorable. For instance, if you're giving someone a book, pair it with a candle that evokes the scent of a cozy library. If you're gifting a homemade meal, include a playlist of their favorite songs to play during dinner.

3. **Capture the Moment**
   Documenting the moment of surprise can add to its longevity. A candid photo or video of the recipient's reaction serves as a tangible reminder of the joy they felt. It's not about staging a perfect moment—it's about preserving the genuine emotions that arise.

4. **Involve Others**
   Collaborative surprises can amplify the emotional impact. For instance, if you're planning a surprise party, involve mutual friends or family members to create a sense of community and shared joy. The collective effort makes the surprise even more meaningful.

5. **Focus on Meaning Over Value**
   The monetary value of a gift is far less important than the thought and effort behind it. A surprise that reflects gen-

uine care and consideration will always outweigh a gift chosen purely for its price tag. It's the meaning behind the gesture that makes it unforgettable.

When Surprise Goes Wrong

While surprises are powerful, they can backfire if not executed thoughtfully. Common pitfalls include:

- Giving a gift that feels inappropriate or irrelevant.
- Overcomplicating the surprise to the point where it becomes stressful or confusing.
- Ignoring the recipient's preferences—some people dislike being the center of attention and may feel uncomfortable with extravagant surprises.

To avoid these missteps, always prioritize the recipient's comfort and preferences over the desire to impress.

The Ripple Effect of a Thoughtful Surprise

A well-executed surprise doesn't just create a moment of joy; it can have a ripple effect. The recipient is likely to share their experience with others, spreading positivity and inspiring others to think more deeply about their own acts of giving. In this way, the art of surprise becomes a gift that keeps on giving.

By mastering the art of surprise, you're not just giving a gift—you're creating an experience, a memory, and a lasting emotional connection. As you move through this book, keep this foundational principle in mind: a great gift is one that surprises, delights, and stays with the recipient long after the moment has passed.

Chapter 2: Why We Gift: The Psychology Behind Generosity

At first glance, gifting may seem like a simple act: you give someone something they want or need. But beneath this seemingly straightforward exchange lies a deeply rooted psychological process. Gifting is an act of connection, one that fulfills fundamental human needs for belonging, recognition, and emotional bonding. This chapter delves into the human drive to give and receive, unpacking the psychology behind generosity and exploring how thoughtful gifts have the power to strengthen relationships in profound ways.

The Human Need to Give and Receive

Gifting is as old as humanity itself, with evidence of its presence in ancient cultures dating back thousands of years. Anthropologists suggest that gifting initially served practical purposes, such as fostering alliances, demonstrating social status, or ensuring mutual survival. Over time, however, gifting evolved into a complex ritual that transcends material value and becomes a symbolic act of connection.

1. **Giving as a Form of Communication**

    Gifts are a language of their own, a way to express emotions that might otherwise go unspoken. Love, gratitude, respect, apology, or celebration—gifts allow us to communicate these sentiments in tangible ways. The act of giving says, "I value you," without the need for words.

2. **The Cycle of Reciprocity**

    Sociologists often describe human relationships as rooted in a cycle of reciprocity: we give, we receive, and this exchange fosters trust and mutual understanding. Gifts play a critical role in this cycle. When we give a thoughtful gift, we not only strengthen our bond with the recipient but also create an opportunity for them to reciprocate, deepening the relationship further.

3. **The Biology of Generosity**

    Neuroscience reveals that giving is biologically rewarding. When we give, our brains release oxytocin, often referred to as the "bonding hormone," which promotes feelings of connection and trust. Additionally, acts of generosity activate the brain's reward center, releasing dopamine and endorphins—chemicals associated with happiness and pleasure. This explains why giving often feels as fulfilling, if not more so, than receiving.

4. **Fulfilling a Need for Belonging**

   Humans are inherently social beings, and our sense of well-being is closely tied to our relationships. Giving allows us to reinforce our place within a community or social group. Whether it's a birthday gift for a friend or a charitable donation to a cause, the act of giving affirms our role as contributors to something larger than ourselves.

The Science of How Thoughtful Gifts Strengthen Relationships

While all gifts carry the potential to impact relationships, thoughtful gifts hold a special kind of power. These are the gifts that demonstrate not just effort but also a deep understanding of the recipient—gifts that make the recipient feel seen, valued, and appreciated. The following are ways in which thoughtful gifting can strengthen bonds:

1. **Enhancing Emotional Intimacy**
   Thoughtful gifts show that you've paid attention to the recipient's likes, needs, and personality. This level of attentiveness communicates care and consideration, which are essential for building emotional intimacy. For example, giving someone a handmade item related to a shared memory can evoke strong feelings of connection.
2. **Building Trust**
   Trust is the cornerstone of any strong relationship, and gifting can reinforce this trust. When you give a gift that reflects the recipient's values or desires, it demonstrates reliability and emotional investment in the relationship. It says, "I know you, and I'm here for you."
3. **Repairing Relationships**
   Gifts can also serve as powerful tools for reconciliation. A well-chosen gift, accompanied by genuine effort, can mend misunderstandings or conflicts. The thoughtfulness behind the gift can signal a desire to move forward and strengthen the relationship.
4. **Creating Shared Joy**
   The act of giving and receiving a thoughtful gift creates a moment of shared joy. This shared emotional experience can strengthen the bond between giver and recipient, turning a simple gesture into a cherished memory. The joy extends beyond the gift itself, creating a positive association with the relationship.

Why We Feel Good When We Give

It's no coincidence that giving feels good—it's wired into our biology and psychology. Researchers have identified several reasons why the act of giving brings happiness:

1. **The Helper's High**
   Similar to the "runner's high" experienced during exercise, giving can produce a euphoric feeling known as the helper's high. This sensation is driven by the release of endorphins, which create a sense of well-being and satisfaction.
2. **A Sense of Purpose**
   Giving helps us feel connected to a larger purpose, whether it's strengthening personal relationships or contributing to a cause. This sense of purpose is a key driver of happiness and fulfillment.
3. **Social Approval and Self-Image**
   Giving enhances our self-image and social standing. While the best gifts are given with genuine intentions, the positive reinforcement we receive—whether it's gratitude from the recipient or admiration from others—can boost our self-esteem and reinforce prosocial behavior.
4. **Anticipation of Joy**
   The act of planning and preparing a thoughtful gift is itself a source of happiness. Imagining the recipient's reaction creates a sense of anticipation and excitement, which adds to the overall joy of giving.

Practical Applications: How to Use Generosity to Strengthen Your Relationships

1. **Be Present in Your Giving**
   Generosity is most impactful when it comes with your presence—both physical and emotional. Take the time to truly engage with the recipient during the gifting moment. A heartfelt explanation of why you chose the gift can make it even more meaningful.
2. **Listen and Observe**
   Thoughtful gifting begins with active listening and observation. Pay attention to the recipient's interests, challenges, and dreams. What do they talk about most? What excites them or brings them joy? These clues can guide you toward the perfect gift.
3. **Make It About Them**
   The most effective gifts are those that prioritize the recipient's preferences over your own. Resist the urge to choose something you'd like for yourself; instead, focus on what will resonate with them.
4. **Celebrate the Little Things**
   Don't wait for major milestones to give a gift. Small, unexpected gestures can often have a greater impact than grandiose offerings tied to big occasions. These "just because" gifts demonstrate ongoing care and attention.
5. **Incorporate Shared Experiences**
   Gifts that create opportunities for shared experiences—such as tickets to an event or a day trip—can strengthen your bond by building new memories together.

The Ripple Effect of Generosity

When we give thoughtfully, the impact extends far beyond the recipient. The joy and gratitude sparked by a meaningful gift can inspire others to act with kindness and generosity, creating a ripple effect of positive energy. Thoughtful gifting strengthens not only individual relationships but also the broader social fabric, fostering a culture of connection and compassion.

Conclusion

The act of giving is deeply rooted in our humanity, and thoughtful gifts have the power to transform relationships. By understanding the psychology behind generosity and learning to give with intention, we can create moments of joy, connection, and lasting impact. As you continue reading this book, remember this foundational truth: the greatest gifts are not about material value—they are about the thought, care, and love that go into them. Thoughtful giving is an art, and when practiced well, it becomes a gift in itself.

Chapter 3: Breaking the Rules: Redefining the Perfect Gift

Traditional gift-giving is often driven by societal norms, convenience, or obligation. Birthdays call for cards and candles, weddings for toasters, and holidays for the latest gadgets. While these gifts are appreciated, they can often feel uninspired, generic, or forgettable. In this chapter, we'll explore why conventional approaches to gifting often fall flat and how redefining the "perfect gift" can transform the act of giving into something truly meaningful and unforgettable.

Why Traditional Gift-Giving Often Falls Flat

1. **Lack of Personal Connection**

   Many traditional gifts are chosen based on generic expectations rather than a deep understanding of the recipient. A scented candle, while pleasant, may not resonate if it doesn't align with the recipient's preferences. These "safe" choices often fail to create a meaningful emotional connection.

2. **Overemphasis on Material Value**

   Society has conditioned us to believe that more expensive gifts equate to better gifts. However, a high price tag doesn't guarantee thoughtfulness. A costly piece of jewelry might impress initially but can feel impersonal if it doesn't reflect the recipient's taste or personality.

3. **Predictability and Routine**

   Traditional gifting occasions often come with predictable gifts. Receiving the same kind of present year after year diminishes the excitement of the experience. People may smile politely, but the emotional impact is minimal.

4. **Obligation and Last-Minute Choices**

   Many gifts are purchased out of obligation, especially during holidays. This rushed, last-minute approach can result in generic gifts that lack creativity or personal touch, making them forgettable.

5. **Cultural and Social Expectations**
   Cultural norms often dictate what is "appropriate" to give in specific situations. For instance, cash is expected at weddings in some cultures, while others favor household items. While these customs hold significance, they can stifle creativity and personalization in gifting.

Redefining the Perfect Gift

The perfect gift isn't about following rules or meeting societal expectations. It's about creating a moment of connection, surprise, and joy that feels uniquely tailored to the recipient. Here's how to break the rules and think outside the box:

1. **Focus on the Recipient's Passion, Not the Occasion**
   Traditional gifting often centers around the event rather than the individual. Instead, focus on what the recipient truly loves or needs. For example, if someone is passionate about painting, a high-quality set of brushes or a class with a local artist will mean far more than a generic gift card.
2. **Give Experiences, Not Things**
   Physical items are tangible, but experiences often leave a more lasting impact. Think concert tickets, cooking classes, skydiving adventures, or a weekend getaway. Experiences create memories, which are far more enduring than material possessions.
3. **Celebrate the Unexpected**
   Break away from traditional occasions and surprise someone on an ordinary day. A "just because" gift carries an element of surprise that makes it all the more meaningful. Imagine gifting someone their favorite dessert on a random Wednesday, simply to brighten their day.
4. **Think Symbolically**
   Gifts with symbolic meaning often carry greater emotional weight. For instance, a handmade scrapbook chronicling your shared memories can evoke deep feelings of nostalgia and connection. Symbolic gifts show thoughtfulness and effort, making them truly unforgettable.
5. **Personalization Is Key**
   Customization elevates any gift. Whether it's engraving a name

or tailoring a gift to a specific interest, personalization makes the recipient feel uniquely valued. For example, a personalized map highlighting places you've traveled together or a custom playlist of songs that hold special meaning.

How to Think Outside the Box for Truly Memorable Gifts

1. **Observe and Listen**
   People often drop hints about their likes and dislikes without realizing it. Pay attention to casual conversations, social media posts, or even their reactions to other gifts. These clues can guide you toward a gift that feels deeply personal.
2. **Create a Shared Experience**
   Shared experiences strengthen bonds. Instead of giving a physical item, plan an activity you can do together, such as hiking, attending a workshop, or watching a movie marathon of their favorite series. The gift becomes not just the experience but the quality time spent together.
3. **Solve a Problem or Fulfill a Need**
   The most memorable gifts often address a specific need or problem in the recipient's life. For example, if someone struggles with organization, a beautifully designed planner tailored to their lifestyle can be both practical and thoughtful.
4. **DIY Gifts: Handmade with Heart**
   Handmade gifts carry an authenticity that store-bought items often lack. Whether it's baking their favorite cookies, knitting a scarf, or creating a custom piece of art, the effort and love poured into a DIY gift make it priceless.
5. **Leverage Inside Jokes or Shared Memories**
   Gifts that reference a private joke or shared experience show a deep connection. For instance, if you and a friend bonded over a specific TV show, a themed gift like a collectible item or a custom piece of fan art can evoke laughter and nostalgia.

6. **Bundle Small, Thoughtful Items**
   Instead of one large gift, consider bundling several smaller items that reflect the recipient's interests. For example, a "self-care kit" with their favorite tea, a cozy blanket, a book, and a scented candle shows thoughtfulness and attention to detail.
7. **Consider the Presentation**
   How a gift is presented can make a significant difference. Wrapping it creatively or adding a personal note can elevate even a simple gift. For example, a heartfelt letter explaining why you chose the gift adds a layer of emotional depth.

Breaking Free from Rules: Examples of Unique Gifts

- **For the Music Lover:** A playlist of songs that remind you of them, paired with a vintage vinyl record.
- **For the Foodie:** A surprise dinner at a local hidden gem or a cooking class with a renowned chef.
- **For the Adventurer:** A scavenger hunt leading to the final gift or an itinerary for a surprise road trip.
- **For the Minimalist:** A donation made in their name to a cause they care about or a digital subscription to a service they love.
- **For the Sentimental Soul:** A custom star map of a special date in their life, like the night they were born or the day they got married.

The Freedom of Creative Gifting

Breaking the rules of traditional gift-giving frees you from the constraints of societal expectations. It allows you to explore creativity, deepen connections, and create moments of genuine joy. The perfect gift isn't about conforming to what's expected—it's about finding a way to say, "I know you, and I care."

When you step outside the box, you redefine what gifting means, making it less about material exchange and more about emotional resonance. As you embrace these ideas, you'll not only become a more thoughtful giver but also create memories that last a lifetime—for both you and the recipient.

Conclusion

The perfect gift doesn't come from a store shelf; it comes from the heart. By breaking the traditional rules of gifting and embracing creativity, thoughtfulness, and personalization, you can redefine what it means to give. Remember, a truly memorable gift isn't about cost or convention—it's about the connection it fosters and the joy it brings. Let this chapter inspire you to think differently and approach gifting as an art, not an obligation.

Chapter 4: The Gift of Experience

When you think of gifts, physical items are often the first things that come to mind: jewelry, gadgets, clothing, or books. While these can bring temporary happiness, they rarely leave a lasting impression. Experiential gifts, on the other hand, have the power to create memories that last a lifetime. These gifts go beyond material value to offer moments of joy, discovery, and connection. In this chapter, we'll explore why giving experiences often surpasses physical gifts and provide creative ideas for experiential gifting tailored to various personalities.

Why Experiences Create Lasting Joy

1. **The Science of Happiness**

   Research shows that experiences bring more lasting happiness than material possessions. While the excitement of a new object fades as we adapt to it, the memories created by experiences grow in value over time. We reminisce about that unforgettable concert, thrilling adventure, or serene getaway, reliving the joy repeatedly.

2. **Connection and Bonding**

   Experiences are often shared, creating opportunities for deeper connection. Whether it's a family trip, a date night, or an outing with friends, these shared moments strengthen bonds and foster a sense of closeness.

3. **A Break from Routine**

   Experiences offer a chance to step outside the daily grind and try something new. This break from routine not only creates excitement but also broadens horizons, enriching the recipient's life in ways that objects rarely can.

4. **Memories Over Materialism**

   Possessions can clutter our lives, but memories enrich them. An experiential gift focuses on the recipient's well-being and personal growth, leaving a legacy of moments rather than items.

How to Choose the Right Experience

1. **Know Their Passions**
   The key to a meaningful experiential gift is aligning it with the recipient's interests. Are they an adrenaline junkie, a foodie, a history buff, or a nature lover? Understanding their personality and preferences ensures your gift will resonate.
2. **Consider Their Bucket List**
   Think about experiences they've always wanted to try but haven't yet pursued. Gifting them something from their bucket list shows that you've been paying attention and care about their dreams.
3. **Tailor the Experience**
   Personalization matters. Even a common experience, like a spa day, can feel extraordinary if it's tailored to the recipient's preferences, such as their favorite type of massage or a specific location they've mentioned wanting to visit.
4. **Think About Timing**
   The timing of the experience can enhance its impact. A surprise weekend getaway during a stressful period or a cooking class just before they host a dinner party can make the gift even more meaningful.

Creative Examples of Experiential Gifts for Every Personality

1. **For the Adventurer**
   - **Hot Air Balloon Ride:** Perfect for someone who loves breathtaking views and a touch of romance.
   - **Skydiving or Bungee Jumping:** For the ultimate thrill-seeker who loves an adrenaline rush.
   - **Escape Room Challenge:** A fun, team-based activity that combines adventure and problem-solving.
2. **For the Food Lover**
   - **Cooking Class:** Offer a class in their favorite cuisine, like Italian pasta-making or sushi rolling.
   - **Private Chef Experience:** Hire a chef to create a gourmet meal at their home.
   - **Food or Wine Tour:** Arrange a day exploring local vineyards, breweries, or food trucks.
3. **For the Nature Enthusiast**
   - **Camping Trip:** Plan a fully equipped weekend getaway in a scenic national park.
   - **Wildlife Safari:** A guided tour of a nature reserve or sanctuary.
   - **Stargazing Experience:** Gift a telescope and organize a stargazing night under a clear sky.
4. **For the Artist or Creative Soul**
   - **Art Workshop:** A painting, pottery, or photography class tailored to their interests.
   - **Behind-the-Scenes Museum Tour:** A private tour of their favorite museum or gallery.

- **Customized Creative Retreat:** A weekend dedicated to exploring their craft, complete with materials and inspiration.

5. **For the Fitness Enthusiast**
   - **Yoga or Meditation Retreat:** A day or weekend of relaxation and self-care.
   - **Adventure Race Entry:** Sponsor their participation in a Tough Mudder, Spartan Race, or fun run.
   - **Personal Training Session:** A one-on-one session with a fitness coach in a discipline they're passionate about.

6. **For the Romantic Partner**
   - **Couples' Spa Day:** A relaxing day designed for two, complete with massages, facials, and downtime.
   - **Surprise Getaway:** A weekend escape to a cozy cabin, beachside resort, or vibrant city.
   - **Date Night Subscription Box:** A series of pre-planned date nights delivered to their doorstep.

7. **For the Knowledge Seeker**
   - **Masterclass Subscription:** Online classes taught by world-renowned experts in fields they love.
   - **Book Club Membership:** Access to curated books and discussion events.
   - **History Tour:** Tickets to a historical site or an expert-led city walking tour.

8. **For the Music Lover**
   - **Concert Tickets:** Secure seats for their favorite band or musician.
   - **Vinyl Club Membership:** A subscription to receive rare or classic records.
   - **Music Festival Pass:** A full experience at a local or international festival.

9. **For the Family-Oriented Individual**

- **Family Photoshoot:** A professional session to capture memories together.
- **Theme Park Adventure:** A day at a local amusement park for the whole family.
- **Game Night Bundle:** Organize a custom family game night with snacks, games, and fun themes.

10. **For the Workaholic**
    - **Wellness Retreat:** Encourage relaxation with a mindfulness retreat focused on work-life balance.
    - **Office Makeover:** Hire a professional organizer or interior designer to revamp their workspace.
    - **Subscription to a Stress-Relief App:** Such as a meditation or productivity tool.

Presenting an Experiential Gift

The way you present an experiential gift can amplify its impact:

- **Customized Invitations:** Design an invitation that outlines the experience in an exciting way. For example, a mock plane ticket for a surprise getaway or a menu card for a cooking class.
- **Complementary Physical Tokens:** Pair the experience with a small, tangible item. For example, give hiking boots for a camping trip or a wine opener for a wine-tasting event.
- **Create a Mystery:** Build anticipation by giving clues leading up to the experience. For instance, leave a trail of notes that reveal the details piece by piece.

Overcoming Potential Barriers to Experiential Gifting

1. **Scheduling Conflicts**
   To avoid clashes, make the experience flexible. Consider open-date vouchers or experiences that allow for rescheduling.
2. **Budget Concerns**
   Experiences don't have to be extravagant. Even low-cost or DIY experiences, like planning a picnic or organizing a movie marathon, can create lasting joy.
3. **Logistical Challenges**
   Offer to handle all the planning to make the gift stress-free for the recipient.

Conclusion

The gift of experience transcends materialism, focusing on creating moments and memories that endure far longer than any object. By giving an experience, you're offering not just an activity but also an opportunity for joy, growth, and connection. Whether it's an adrenaline-pumping adventure or a serene day of relaxation, experiential gifts leave an indelible mark on the heart and mind. So, think outside the box, dive into the recipient's world, and craft an unforgettable experience that they'll cherish forever.

Chapter 5: The Minimalist Giver

In a world overflowing with stuff, the idea of "less is more" has never been more relevant. As minimalism gains traction as a lifestyle, gifting has also evolved to reflect this ethos. Minimalist gifting focuses on meaningfulness, intentionality, and the elimination of unnecessary clutter. It's about giving something that truly enhances the recipient's life without adding to the physical or mental burden of owning too many things.

This chapter explores why "less is more" when it comes to gifting and provides practical advice on how to give meaningful gifts that align with minimalist principles.

Why "Less Is More" When Choosing Gifts

1. **The Overwhelm of Too Much Stuff**
   Many people already feel burdened by an excess of belongings. Adding to this clutter—even with good intentions—can create more stress than joy. Minimalist gifting acknowledges this reality, focusing on quality over quantity and the emotional impact of a gift over its physical presence.

2. **The Value of Simplicity**
   Minimalist gifts often carry a sense of calm and clarity. By stripping away unnecessary extravagance, these gifts emphasize thoughtfulness and utility. The recipient isn't just given an item—they're given the space to enjoy it without distraction.

3. **Environmental Impact**
   Our consumer culture has a significant ecological footprint. Minimalist gifting reduces waste, encourages sustainability, and aligns with eco-conscious values. Gifts that are durable, reusable, or entirely intangible help protect the planet while still bringing joy.

4. **The Emotional Weight of Possessions**
   Beyond physical clutter, excess possessions can carry emotional weight. Gifts that are unused or unwanted may evoke guilt or

obligation to keep them. Minimalist gifts, chosen with care, avoid this burden by prioritizing the recipient's needs and desires.

Principles of Minimalist Gifting

1. **Intentionality**
   Every gift should have a purpose. Ask yourself: Does this gift enhance the recipient's life? Will it bring them joy, ease, or inspiration? Gifts given with intention are far more meaningful than those chosen out of obligation.
2. **Functionality**
   A minimalist gift often serves a practical purpose, making the recipient's life easier or more enjoyable. Think of items that solve a problem or fulfill a specific need without being overly complex or decorative.
3. **Quality Over Quantity**
   One well-made, thoughtful gift has more impact than several lower-quality items. Minimalist gifting often prioritizes durability and timelessness, ensuring that the gift will be appreciated and used for years to come.
4. **Experiences Over Objects**
   As explored in the previous chapter, experiential gifts often carry greater emotional value than physical items. A minimalist approach leans heavily on experiences that create memories without adding to physical clutter.

How to Give Meaningful Gifts That Don't Clutter Lives

1. **Digital and Subscription-Based Gifts**
   - **E-Books and Audiobooks:** Perfect for book lovers who don't have space for physical copies.
   - **Streaming Subscriptions:** Gift access to music, movies, or TV shows tailored to the recipient's tastes.
   - **Online Learning Platforms:** Classes or courses in a subject they're passionate about, from cooking to coding.
   - **Meditation or Wellness Apps:** Encourage relaxation and mindfulness with a premium subscription.
2. **Consumable Gifts**
   - **Gourmet Food or Drink:** High-quality chocolates, exotic teas, specialty coffees, or artisan snacks make thoughtful gifts that won't linger once consumed.
   - **Homemade Treats:** Bake cookies, craft preserves, or create a personalized spice blend.
   - **Luxurious Self-Care Items:** Gift bath salts, candles, or skincare items that can be used and enjoyed.
3. **Multi-Use or Practical Items**
   - **Reusable Goods:** High-quality water bottles, tote bags, or food storage containers that encourage sustainability.
   - **Minimalist Tools:** Pocket-sized multitools, portable chargers, or versatile kitchen gadgets.
   - **Everyday Essentials:** A set of durable socks, a premium notebook, or a reliable pen—items people use regularly but may not splurge on for themselves.
4. **Shared Experiences**
   - **Tickets to Events:** A concert, play, or sports game tailored to their interests.
   - **Memberships or Passes:** Access to museums, botanical gardens, or fitness classes.

- **Day Trips or Adventures:** Plan a simple, memorable outing like a hike, a visit to a nearby town, or a picnic in a beautiful location.

5. **Customized Gifts**
    - **Personalized Keepsakes:** A photo book, a custom piece of art, or a journal with their name or initials.
    - **Tailored Services:** A gift certificate for a professional organizer, personal trainer, or even a cleaning service.
6. **Eco-Friendly and Sustainable Gifts**
    - **Plant-Based Gifts:** A small indoor plant, a tree planted in their honor, or a seed kit for a garden.
    - **Sustainable Upgrades:** Items like beeswax wraps, solar-powered gadgets, or compostable kitchen tools.

Examples of Minimalist Gifting for Different Personalities

1. **The Tech Enthusiast**
    - A subscription to a premium productivity app.
    - Noise-canceling earbuds.
    - A digital gift card for their favorite software or platform.
2. **The Nature Lover**
    - A National Park pass.
    - A high-quality water filter or portable hammock for camping trips.
    - An eco-friendly bird feeder or bee house.
3. **The Wellness Seeker**
    - A yoga class membership or a mindfulness retreat.
    - A set of organic essential oils.
    - A minimalist journal for gratitude or habit tracking.
4. **The Foodie**
    - A private cooking class.
    - A gourmet olive oil tasting set.
    - A subscription to a meal kit delivery service.

5. **The Busy Professional**
    - A premium planner or productivity tool.
    - A gift certificate for a meal prep service.
    - A portable charger or ergonomic office accessory.

How to Present Minimalist Gifts

1. **Eco-Friendly Wrapping**
   Use reusable materials like cloth wraps, tote bags, or simple kraft paper tied with natural twine.
2. **Digital Presentation**
   For intangible gifts, create a digital card or a visually appealing email that explains the gift. Add a personal touch by including a heartfelt message.
3. **Simple, Elegant Packaging**
   Minimalist gifts benefit from understated presentation. A single ribbon or a sprig of greenery can elevate the unwrapping experience.

The Emotional Impact of Minimalist Giving

Minimalist gifting isn't just about reducing clutter; it's about redefining what it means to give. It shifts the focus from the quantity or cost of the gift to the thoughtfulness behind it. By prioritizing the recipient's needs, values, and lifestyle, minimalist gifts demonstrate care and intentionality, creating deeper emotional connections.

Conclusion

Minimalist gifting is an art of restraint, requiring you to think carefully about what truly matters to the recipient. It challenges the traditional notion that more is better and instead emphasizes the joy of simplicity, utility, and thoughtfulness. By adopting a minimalist approach, you can give gifts that resonate deeply, enhance lives, and leave a lasting impression—without adding to the physical or emotional clutter of the recipient's world.

Chapter 6: The Power of Personalized Giving

Personalized gifts hold a unique power—they speak directly to the recipient in a way that no generic gift can. These gifts transcend the ordinary by showing thoughtfulness, effort, and an intimate understanding of the person they're for. Personalized gifts not only make the recipient feel special but also create lasting memories, as they often reflect shared experiences or personal milestones.

This chapter explores why tailored gifts resonate so deeply and offers practical tips for personalizing gifts that will be cherished and remembered.

Why Personalized Gifts Resonate Deeply

1. **They Show Thoughtfulness and Effort**
   A personalized gift demonstrates that you took the time to consider the recipient's personality, interests, and preferences. This effort shows care and commitment, which deepens the emotional connection between giver and recipient.
2. **They Make People Feel Seen**
   Personalized gifts acknowledge the recipient's individuality. They say, "I see you, and I value what makes you unique." This validation creates a sense of belonging and strengthens relationships.
3. **They Evoke Stronger Emotional Reactions**
   Gifts that reflect a person's life experiences or interests often trigger deeper emotional responses. For example, a customized map of a favorite city they visited or a piece of jewelry engraved with a significant date can bring a flood of positive memories.
4. **They Are Often Timeless**
   While trends come and go, personalized gifts hold timeless value. Because they're tied to the recipient's identity or story, they remain meaningful long after other gifts are forgotten.
5. **They Build and Reinforce Bonds**
   Personalized gifts are a testament to the depth of your relation-

ship. They highlight shared experiences, inside jokes, or specific traits, reinforcing the bond between you and the recipient.

Tips for Personalizing Gifts to Make Them Unforgettable

1. **Start with What You Know**
   Consider the recipient's interests, hobbies, and life milestones. What are their favorite activities, places, or colors? Have they recently achieved a goal or overcome a challenge? Use this information as a foundation for your gift.
   - **Example:** If they love traveling, create a scrapbook of their past trips or gift them a scratch-off map of the world.

2. **Use Shared Memories**
   Incorporate elements of your shared history into the gift. A framed photo from a meaningful event, a playlist of songs tied to your experiences, or a handwritten letter recounting a cherished memory can make the gift uniquely personal.
   - **Example:** For a friend you bonded with over late-night coffee runs, consider a custom mug with an inside joke or a photo from one of those nights.

3. **Customize with Names, Dates, or Messages**
   Adding a name, date, or meaningful quote to an item transforms it into something truly one-of-a-kind. Many services allow you to engrave, embroider, or print custom text on items like jewelry, clothing, or home decor.
   - **Example:** A leather-bound journal engraved with their initials and a motivational quote they love.

4. **Incorporate Their Personality**
   Tailor the gift to their unique traits. Are they quirky, sentimental, adventurous, or pragmatic? Align the gift with their personality to ensure it resonates.

- **Example:** For someone with a quirky sense of humor, a custom cartoon portrait of them and their pet might be perfect.

5. **Choose Practical Personalization**

   Personalized gifts don't have to be purely decorative. Functional items that reflect the recipient's personality are both meaningful and practical.
   - **Example:** A monogrammed tote bag for someone who's always on the go or a custom recipe box for a budding chef.

6. **Leverage Technology**

   Today's digital tools make personalization easier than ever. Many platforms offer customizable options for gifts like photo books, calendars, and even 3D-printed keepsakes.
   - **Example:** Use an online service to create a custom star map of the night they were born or another significant date.

7. **Make It Interactive**

   Gifts that require the recipient's participation can be deeply engaging. Consider items that they can personalize further or experiences that invite their input.
   - **Example:** A build-your-own gift set, like a spice kit for a home cook or a DIY terrarium for a plant enthusiast.

8. **Include a Personal Note or Story**

   Even the simplest gift can become extraordinary when accompanied by a heartfelt note explaining why you chose it. Share the story behind the gift or the meaning it holds.
   - **Example:** If you gift someone a necklace with a specific charm, include a note explaining what the charm symbolizes and why it reminded you of them.

9. **Think Beyond Physical Gifts**

   Personalization isn't limited to tangible items. Personalized experiences, such as a curated day trip, a surprise dinner, or a bespoke playlist, can be just as impactful.

- **Example:** Plan a "day of favorites" where every activity, meal, and location is tailored to their preferences.

10. **Pay Attention to Presentation**

    The way a personalized gift is presented can amplify its impact. Creative wrapping, a handwritten tag, or a unique unboxing experience adds an extra layer of thoughtfulness.

- **Example:** For a custom scarf, wrap it in a vintage-style box with a handwritten note describing why you chose the colors or pattern.

Examples of Personalized Gifts for Different Situations

1. **For a Milestone Celebration**
   - A custom timeline or photo collage showcasing their journey.
   - An engraved watch or piece of jewelry with a date and message.
2. **For a Romantic Partner**
   - A personalized book recounting your love story.
   - A custom piece of artwork inspired by a shared experience.
3. **For a Close Friend**
   - A set of items tailored to an inside joke or shared hobby.
   - A customized journal with prompts related to their passions.
4. **For a Family Member**
   - A family tree print with photos and names.
   - A recipe book filled with family recipes and notes.
5. **For a Colleague or Acquaintance**
   - A personalized desk accessory, like a pen or notebook.
   - A custom thank-you card or digital gift card for their favorite store.

Common Mistakes to Avoid in Personalized Giving

1. **Focusing Only on Trends**
   Just because a personalized item is popular doesn't mean it will resonate with your recipient. Make sure it aligns with their unique preferences and not just current fads.
2. **Overdoing It**
   Personalization should enhance the gift, not overwhelm it. Avoid cramming too many names, dates, or messages onto an item. Subtlety often has a greater impact.
3. **Ignoring Practicality**
   A highly personalized item might look great but have limited use. Ensure that your gift is not only meaningful but also practical for the recipient.
4. **Forgetting the Recipient's Style**
   Not everyone likes bold or flashy personalization. Match the gift's design to their aesthetic—minimalist, colorful, vintage, etc.

The Lasting Impact of Personalized Gifts

Personalized gifts have an unparalleled ability to create emotional connections. They're a testament to the time and thought you've invested in the relationship, making the recipient feel truly valued. These gifts go beyond material value to become treasured keepsakes, often evoking fond memories years later.

By embracing personalization, you're not just giving a gift—you're giving a part of yourself. Each tailored detail, shared memory, or meaningful message strengthens your bond with the recipient, ensuring the gift is as unforgettable as the sentiment behind it.

Conclusion

The power of personalized giving lies in its ability to transcend the ordinary and create something deeply meaningful. By tailoring gifts to reflect the recipient's unique traits, shared memories, or passions, you elevate the act of giving into an art form. Thoughtful personalization isn't about extravagance—it's about understanding, effort, and connection. As you embrace the principles and practices of personalized giving, you'll find that the most cherished gifts are those that speak directly to the heart.

Chapter 7: When the Gift Is You

In our fast-paced, material-driven world, we often overlook the most meaningful and valuable gift we can give—ourselves. Time, presence, and emotional availability are gifts that can't be bought or wrapped but often mean more than any tangible item. This chapter delves into the profound impact of offering your time and presence to those you care about and illustrates through real-life stories how "being there" can make all the difference.

The Ultimate Gift: Time, Presence, and Emotional Availability

1. **The Gift of Time**
   Time is our most finite resource, making it an incredibly valuable gift. Spending quality time with someone shows that you prioritize them above all else. Whether it's an afternoon together, a phone call, or simply sitting in silence, your time is a direct expression of care and commitment.
2. **The Gift of Presence**
   Presence is about being fully engaged and mindful in the moment. It means putting aside distractions—turning off your phone, setting aside work, and truly focusing on the person in front of you. When you give your presence, you create a space for genuine connection.
3. **The Gift of Emotional Availability**
   Emotional availability goes beyond physical presence. It's about being open, empathetic, and attuned to the other person's feelings and needs. Whether you're offering a listening ear, a shoulder to lean on, or heartfelt words of encouragement, emotional support fosters deeper bonds and understanding.

Why "Being There" Matters More Than Things

1. **The Human Need for Connection**
   At their core, people crave connection and belonging. Material gifts may provide temporary satisfaction, but it's the shared experiences and emotional bonds that leave lasting impressions. Being there for someone fulfills this intrinsic need.
2. **Moments That Can't Be Replaced**
   Life is full of fleeting moments—birthdays, graduations, weddings, and even quiet evenings together. These moments can't be recreated, and your presence during these times often means more than any gift you could buy.
3. **Support During Difficult Times**
   During life's challenges, what people need most isn't objects but support. Being there for someone in their darkest moments—a hospital visit, a funeral, or simply sitting with them in their grief—demonstrates a depth of care that words or gifts can't convey.
4. **The Legacy of Shared Memories**
   Years down the line, people may forget what you gave them, but they'll always remember how you made them feel. By prioritizing presence over presents, you create a legacy of love and connection that endures.

How to Make Yourself the Gift

1. **Prioritize Quality Time**
    - **Plan Intentional Moments:** Set aside dedicated time for your loved ones, whether it's a weekend getaway, a long walk, or a simple dinner at home.
    - **Be Fully Present:** Give them your undivided attention by removing distractions and focusing on the moment.
2. **Offer Acts of Service**
    - Help with a project they've been struggling with, offer to babysit their kids, or assist with chores. Acts of service show care through action rather than words or material goods.
3. **Be a Source of Emotional Support**
    - Be an active listener when they need to talk. Offer empathy and understanding without judgment.
    - Celebrate their victories and stand by them during setbacks.
4. **Be There for Milestones**
    - Attend their important events—graduations, performances, anniversaries. Your presence at these milestones demonstrates that you value their accomplishments and joy.
5. **Create Shared Experiences**
    - Suggest activities you can enjoy together, from hiking and cooking to exploring a museum or taking a class. The time spent together becomes the gift itself.
6. **Surprise Them with Your Time**
    - Show up unexpectedly for a loved one who's far away, plan a spontaneous visit, or take them on a surprise outing. These moments are often unforgettable.

Real-Life Stories: How "Being There" Made All the Difference

1. **The Grandparent's Joy**
   Emma's grandparents lived hours away, and she struggled to visit them often. For their 50th wedding anniversary, instead of sending a gift, Emma surprised them by driving to their house unannounced. She spent the weekend listening to their stories, flipping through old photo albums, and cooking dinner together. Years later, after her grandparents had passed, Emma reflected on how those simple hours meant more to them—and to her—than any material gift could.

2. **A Friend in Need**
   After losing his job, Carlos fell into a deep depression. While others sent cards or text messages, his best friend, Noah, showed up at his door with coffee and a willingness to sit and listen. Over several weeks, Noah made a point of spending time with Carlos, offering encouragement and practical help like revising his resume. Years later, Carlos often mentioned how Noah's consistent presence gave him the strength to rebuild his life.

3. **The Surprise Graduation**
   Maya's parents couldn't afford to travel to her college graduation, which was several states away. Unbeknownst to her, her older brother saved up and arranged for their parents to fly in. Seeing her family in the audience as she crossed the stage brought Maya to tears. She later said their presence made her achievement feel truly complete.

4. **A Community of Care**
   When Sarah's house was damaged by a flood, her neighbors didn't just send condolences—they showed up. They spent days helping her clean, salvage belongings, and rebuild. Sarah often remarked that their presence turned a devastating experience into one where she felt supported and cared for.

5. **Reconnecting Through Time**
   After years of a strained relationship, Andrew decided to spend a week with his father at his rural cabin. During that time, they fished, cooked, and talked—really talked—for the first time in years. That week became the turning point in their relationship, reminding Andrew that his time and presence could heal wounds that words couldn't.

How to Foster a Culture of Presence

1. **Prioritize Relationships Over Things**
   Shift your mindset to value shared time and emotional connection over material gifts. Make it a habit to invest in people rather than possessions.
2. **Express Gratitude Regularly**
   Let people know how much their presence means to you. Small gestures, like a heartfelt "thank you" or a note expressing appreciation, reinforce the value of being there for one another.
3. **Be Intentional About Giving Your Time**
   Whether it's setting regular coffee dates with a friend, calling a loved one weekly, or making time for family dinners, consistency shows that you care.
4. **Practice Active Listening**
   Being present doesn't just mean showing up—it means truly hearing and understanding the other person. Put aside distractions and engage fully in conversations.

The Ripple Effect of Your Presence

When you give your time and presence to others, it creates a ripple effect. The connections you strengthen inspire those around you to do the same, fostering a culture of care and community. In a world that often values things over people, choosing to be present is a radical act of love and humanity.

Conclusion

The greatest gifts aren't wrapped in ribbons or boxes—they're found in moments of connection, shared laughter, and unwavering support. By giving your time, presence, and emotional availability, you offer something far more valuable than material items. You become the gift, creating bonds and memories that last a lifetime. In the end, what people will remember most isn't what you gave them—it's that you were there.

Chapter 8: Gifts That Heal

Gifts have the power to do more than bring joy—they can comfort, inspire, and help someone navigate through life's challenges. During difficult times, the right gift becomes a tangible expression of empathy and support, offering solace when words may fall short. In this chapter, we'll explore how thoughtful, restorative gifts can heal emotional wounds, inspire resilience, and foster connection. We'll also discuss how emotional intelligence plays a crucial role in selecting these gifts.

The Healing Power of Gifts

1. **A Beacon of Hope**
   During tough times, a well-chosen gift can serve as a symbol of hope and encouragement. It reminds the recipient that they're not alone and that brighter days are ahead. For instance, a journal to process emotions or a plant to nurture can symbolize growth and renewal.

2. **A Physical Manifestation of Care**
   When someone is grieving, anxious, or struggling, a gift can become a physical reminder of your presence and support. Whether it's a soft blanket, a heartfelt letter, or a small token of remembrance, these items provide comfort and reassurance.

3. **A Catalyst for Healing**
   Certain gifts can actively aid in the healing process, whether through self-care, creative expression, or physical well-being. For example, a mindfulness book or a spa kit encourages relaxation and introspection.

4. **A Way to Honor Emotions**
   Healing gifts often acknowledge the recipient's pain or struggle without attempting to "fix" it. They validate feelings and provide a gentle way to navigate through them.

Emotional Intelligence in Choosing Restorative Gifts

1. **Listen and Observe**
   Emotional intelligence begins with active listening and observation. Pay attention to what the person says—or doesn't say. Their words, behaviors, and emotional state can provide valuable clues about what they need most.
   - **Example:** If someone often mentions feeling overwhelmed, a calming tea set or a mindfulness coloring book might help.
2. **Acknowledge, Don't Assume**
   Avoid making assumptions about what the person needs. Instead, acknowledge their feelings with open-ended questions or thoughtful comments, such as:
   - "I know you're going through a lot right now. Is there anything that might make things a little easier?"
   - "I wanted to give you something to remind you that you're not alone."
3. **Consider Their Personality and Preferences**
   A healing gift should align with the recipient's personality. Are they introverted or extroverted? Do they enjoy creative outlets, physical activities, or quiet reflection? Tailoring the gift to their preferences ensures it resonates.
   - **Example:** An extrovert might appreciate tickets to a restorative yoga class, while an introvert might prefer a cozy reading nook setup.
4. **Prioritize Practicality**
   During tough times, practical gifts can provide immense relief. These might include meal delivery services, grocery gift cards, or childcare help. These gestures lighten the load and demonstrate a deep understanding of their situation.

5. **Be Genuine and Sincere**

   The intention behind the gift matters as much as the gift itself. Avoid anything that feels performative or obligatory. A genuine, heartfelt gesture carries far more weight than a flashy or expensive item.

Types of Restorative Gifts

1. **Gifts That Comfort**
   - **Blankets or Throws:** A soft, cozy blanket provides warmth and a sense of security.
   - **Aromatherapy Diffusers:** Essential oils like lavender or eucalyptus promote relaxation and calm.
   - **Weighted Blankets:** Known for their therapeutic effects, these blankets can reduce anxiety and improve sleep.
2. **Gifts That Inspire**
   - **Inspirational Books:** Choose titles with uplifting themes or motivational messages.
   - **Art Supplies:** Encourage creative expression with a sketchbook, paints, or a crafting kit.
   - **Personalized Items:** A custom piece of jewelry with an inspirational quote or their name can serve as a daily reminder of resilience.
3. **Gifts That Support Self-Care**
   - **Spa Kits:** Include bath salts, candles, and skincare items to encourage relaxation.
   - **Fitness Passes:** A yoga or meditation class can provide physical and mental renewal.
   - **Guided Journals:** Prompts for gratitude, reflection, or goal-setting help the recipient process emotions.
4. **Gifts That Honor Loss**
   - **Memory Boxes:** A place to store keepsakes and mementos of a loved one.
   - **Personalized Memorials:** Engraved items, such as a pendant with a loved one's handwriting, can offer comfort.

- **Donation in Their Name:** Contributing to a cause meaningful to the recipient or their loved one can be deeply healing.
5. **Gifts That Offer Practical Help**
    - **Meal Delivery Services:** Provide sustenance and reduce the burden of cooking.
    - **Cleaning Services:** Help them regain a sense of order in their home.
    - **Subscription Boxes:** Monthly deliveries of self-care items, snacks, or books bring ongoing moments of joy.

Creative Ways to Present Healing Gifts

1. **Include a Personal Note**
   A handwritten letter explaining why you chose the gift adds a layer of meaning. Express your support, share a comforting memory, or offer words of encouragement.
    - **Example:** "I thought of you when I saw this journal. I hope it helps you process your thoughts and feelings, just as you've helped me with mine."
2. **Bundle with Intention**
   Create a gift package with a theme, such as relaxation or renewal. For example, pair a weighted blanket with herbal tea and a mindfulness book for a "restorative evening" kit.
3. **Use Thoughtful Wrapping**
   Present the gift in a way that feels comforting and special. A reusable cloth bag, a wooden box, or even simple kraft paper with a sprig of greenery can add a touch of care.
4. **Deliver It in Person**
   If possible, deliver the gift yourself. Your presence adds another layer of comfort and connection, turning the act of giving into a shared experience.

Real-Life Stories: Gifts That Made a Difference

1. **A Journal for Healing**
   After losing her mother, Maria's best friend gave her a guided grief journal with prompts to help her process her emotions. Alongside the journal was a pen engraved with her mother's name. Maria later shared that the gift gave her a safe space to explore her feelings and feel connected to her mother's memory.
2. **Meals in Times of Crisis**
   When Jack's wife was hospitalized unexpectedly, his coworkers banded together to arrange a month of meal deliveries. The practical support not only eased Jack's stress but also reminded him that he wasn't alone during a challenging time.
3. **A Trip Down Memory Lane**
   When Sarah's best friend moved across the country, Sarah gifted her a scrapbook filled with photos, tickets, and notes from their years of friendship. Each page included a letter Sarah had written, recounting a memory and what it meant to her. Sarah's friend said the scrapbook became her anchor during lonely moments.
4. **A Plant for New Beginnings**
   After recovering from a long illness, Emma received a small, easy-to-care-for plant from a colleague with a note saying, "May this grow alongside your strength." The plant became a symbol of Emma's recovery, reminding her of her resilience and her colleague's thoughtfulness.

Conclusion

Gifts that heal are more than just gestures—they are lifelines, symbols of hope, and reminders of love. By using emotional intelligence and deep care in your choices, you can offer solace, inspire resilience, and provide a sense of connection during life's most difficult times. When the right gift speaks to the heart, it becomes a powerful force for healing, reminding the recipient that they are seen, valued, and never alone.

Chapter 9: The Joy of Giving for the Sake of Giving

True generosity comes from giving without expecting anything in return. It's not about reciprocation, recognition, or reward—it's about the pure joy of bringing happiness to others. This kind of selfless giving strengthens relationships, fosters trust, and creates ripples of positivity that can transform not only the recipient's life but also your own. In this chapter, we'll explore the profound impact of giving for its own sake and provide simple, actionable ways to practice generosity in everyday life.

How Giving Without Expectations Can Transform Relationships

1. **Fostering Authentic Connections**
   When you give without expecting anything in return, you create an atmosphere of trust and authenticity. The recipient feels valued for who they are, not for what they can provide in return. This deepens bonds and strengthens relationships.
2. **Demonstrating Unconditional Care**
   Giving selflessly communicates that your care and support are not contingent on any conditions. This kind of generosity shows others that your actions stem from genuine kindness, reinforcing emotional safety and security in the relationship.
3. **Encouraging a Ripple Effect**
   Acts of selfless giving inspire others to do the same. When someone experiences generosity without strings attached, they're often moved to pass it on, creating a chain reaction of kindness that can impact countless lives.
4. **Reducing Resentment and Misunderstandings**
   Giving with expectations can sometimes lead to resentment or disappointment if those expectations aren't met. By giving selflessly, you eliminate these risks, ensuring the gift is purely a source of joy and connection.

5. **Reaping Emotional Rewards**
   Research shows that giving activates areas of the brain associated with pleasure and satisfaction. The act of giving for its own sake not only benefits the recipient but also enhances your emotional well-being.

The Psychological Benefits of Selfless Giving

1. **Boosts Mental Health**
   Giving can reduce stress, anxiety, and depression by shifting the focus away from personal challenges and onto the well-being of others. It fosters a sense of purpose and connection, which are critical for mental health.
2. **Strengthens Empathy**
   Selfless giving encourages you to consider the needs and feelings of others, cultivating empathy and compassion. This mindset enriches relationships and fosters a deeper understanding of the people around you.
3. **Enhances Gratitude**
   The act of giving often highlights what you have to offer, fostering a sense of gratitude for your own life and resources. Gratitude, in turn, boosts happiness and resilience.
4. **Promotes a Growth Mindset**
   Generosity encourages you to think expansively. By giving freely, you embrace the idea that resources—whether material, emotional, or time—are abundant, fostering a mindset of growth rather than scarcity.

Simple Acts of Generosity That Create Ripples of Joy

1. **Unexpected Kindness**
    - Pay for the coffee of the person behind you in line.
    - Leave an encouraging note on a coworker's desk.
    - Compliment a stranger on something you genuinely admire.
2. **Give Your Time**
    - Volunteer at a local shelter, library, or community center.
    - Spend an afternoon helping a friend with a project or task.
    - Visit someone who might feel isolated, like an elderly neighbor or a friend recovering from illness.
3. **Share Your Skills**
    - Offer to teach someone a skill you excel at, such as cooking, gardening, or a software program.
    - Help a student with their homework or mentor a junior colleague.
4. **Support Local Causes**
    - Donate to a local charity or fund a community project.
    - Purchase from small businesses or artisans to support their livelihood.
    - Organize a donation drive for essentials like food, clothing, or school supplies.
5. **Create Moments of Joy**
    - Surprise a loved one with a small gift or treat, like their favorite snack or a handwritten letter.
    - Plan a spontaneous outing with a friend who might need a break.

- Host a casual gathering just to bring people together for laughter and connection.

6. **Be a Listening Ear**
    - Take the time to listen to someone without offering advice unless they ask for it.
    - Acknowledge their feelings and validate their experiences, creating a safe space for them to share.

7. **Pay It Forward**
    - Leave a generous tip for a server or delivery person.
    - Donate books, toys, or clothes to those in need.
    - Cover a stranger's parking meter or bus fare.

8. **Small Gestures with Big Impact**
    - Bring flowers or baked goods to a teacher, nurse, or public servant to thank them for their hard work.
    - Offer to babysit for a busy parent so they can have some time to relax.
    - Pick up litter during a walk to improve your community's environment.

Real-Life Stories: The Power of Selfless Giving

1. **The Anonymous Donor**
   In a small town, a struggling single mother found a gift card for groceries in her mailbox one day. It came with a note: "You're not alone. Take care of yourself and your family." The act of kindness inspired her to volunteer at a food bank once she got back on her feet, paying the kindness forward.
2. **A Gift of Presence**
   When James's friend was grieving the loss of a parent, James didn't know what to say or do. Instead of offering advice, he showed up with their favorite board game and simply spent the evening playing and reminiscing about good times. His friend later said it was the first moment they felt truly comforted since the loss.
3. **A Stranger's Act of Kindness**
   On a rainy day, an elderly man struggled to load groceries into his car. A young woman nearby stopped to help, offering her umbrella to shield him from the rain. The man thanked her and said, "You've restored my faith in people today." That simple act brightened both of their days.
4. **Transforming a Classroom**
   A teacher, overwhelmed with outdated supplies, mentioned it in passing to a neighbor. A week later, the neighbor rallied a group of parents and donated art supplies, books, and educational games to the class. The teacher shared that it reignited her passion for teaching and made a significant impact on her students.

How to Cultivate a Habit of Giving for Its Own Sake

1. **Start Small**
   Generosity doesn't have to involve grand gestures. Begin with small acts of kindness in your daily life, such as holding the door open or smiling at a stranger.
2. **Incorporate Giving into Your Routine**
   Make generosity a regular part of your life. Set aside time weekly or monthly to engage in acts of kindness, whether volunteering, donating, or helping a friend.
3. **Focus on the Recipient's Joy**
   Shift your mindset to prioritize the recipient's happiness. Instead of wondering what you'll get in return, focus on the positive impact your actions will have on them.
4. **Reflect on the Benefits**
   After each act of giving, take a moment to reflect on how it made you feel and how it impacted the recipient. This reinforces the intrinsic value of generosity.

The Ripple Effect of Generosity

When you give selflessly, you inspire others to do the same. The ripple effect of generosity can transform communities, workplaces, and relationships. Acts of kindness spread positivity, creating a culture of care and connection that benefits everyone involved.

Conclusion

Giving for the sake of giving is one of the purest expressions of humanity. By offering your time, resources, and kindness without expecting anything in return, you strengthen relationships, uplift others, and enrich your own life. The joy of selfless giving is that it not only transforms the recipient but also creates a ripple effect of goodwill that extends far beyond the initial act. In the end, generosity is its own reward, reminding us all of the profound beauty in simply giving.

Chapter 10: The Universal Gift List

Finding the perfect gift can be a daunting task, especially when you're unsure of the recipient's tastes or interests. However, some gifts transcend individual preferences, appealing to a wide range of people regardless of age, background, or personality. These timeless gifts are versatile, meaningful, and practical, making them go-to options for any occasion.

This chapter presents a curated list of universal gifts, explaining why they resonate so well and why they almost never fail. Whether for a friend, colleague, family member, or even a casual acquaintance, these suggestions are designed to bring joy and leave a lasting impression.

What Makes a Gift Universal?

1. **Practicality**
   Universal gifts are often functional, making them useful in everyday life. A practical gift solves a problem or meets a need, ensuring it won't end up collecting dust.
2. **Versatility**
   These gifts appeal to a broad audience because they don't rely on specific tastes or preferences. They fit seamlessly into various lifestyles and situations.
3. **Timelessness**
   Unlike trendy or niche items, universal gifts have enduring appeal. They're not tied to a particular season, fad, or cultural moment, making them suitable for anyone, anytime.
4. **Emotional Resonance**
   Many universal gifts carry intrinsic meaning or foster positive emotions, such as comfort, appreciation, or joy. They often have a personal touch that enhances their value.
5. **Inclusivity**
   These gifts avoid being overly specific or exclusive, making them

appropriate for a diverse range of recipients, from children to seniors, and across cultural or professional settings.

The Universal Gift List

1. **Books**
   - **Why They Work:** Books are versatile and meaningful, offering entertainment, knowledge, or inspiration. A general-interest book, such as a bestselling novel, a motivational guide, or a coffee table book, can appeal to almost anyone.
   - **Examples:**
     - A beautifully illustrated cookbook.
     - A self-help or personal growth book.
     - A universally loved classic novel like *To Kill a Mockingbird*.
2. **Gift Cards**
   - **Why They Work:** Gift cards offer flexibility, allowing recipients to choose something they genuinely want or need. They're especially appreciated when you're unsure of the recipient's preferences.
   - **Examples:**
     - Amazon or major retail store gift cards.
     - Dining gift cards for popular chain restaurants or food delivery services.
     - Digital gift cards for streaming platforms like Netflix or Spotify.
3. **High-Quality Notebooks or Journals**
   - **Why They Work:** A stylish notebook or journal is practical, personal, and universally appreciated. It can be used for jotting down ideas, journaling, or organizing tasks.
   - **Examples:**
     - A leather-bound journal.
     - A minimalist planner.

- A gratitude journal with prompts.

4. **Candles**
    - **Why They Work:** Scented candles create a cozy, inviting atmosphere and are perfect for relaxation. Opt for neutral scents to appeal to a broader audience.
    - **Examples:**
        - Vanilla, lavender, or citrus-scented candles.
        - A set of tealight candles with decorative holders.
        - A long-burning soy wax candle in elegant packaging.

5. **Blankets or Throws**
    - **Why They Work:** A soft, high-quality blanket provides warmth and comfort, making it a universally appreciated gift.
    - **Examples:**
        - A plush fleece throw.
        - A weighted blanket for relaxation.
        - A luxurious wool or cashmere blend blanket.

6. **Plants or Succulents**
    - **Why They Work:** Plants bring a touch of nature into any space and are simple enough to care for, even for those without a green thumb.
    - **Examples:**
        - Low-maintenance succulents like jade plants or echeverias.
        - A small potted herb garden (basil, mint, rosemary).
        - An air-purifying plant like a snake plant or pothos.

7. **Reusable Water Bottles or Tumblers**
    - **Why They Work:** Sustainable, eco-friendly gifts like water bottles are practical for everyone and promote healthier habits.
    - **Examples:**
        - Insulated stainless steel water bottles.
        - Tumblers with built-in straws for cold drinks.

- A sleek, reusable coffee mug.

8. **Food and Treats**
   - **Why They Work:** Gourmet treats are a safe bet because almost everyone enjoys indulging in high-quality snacks or beverages.
   - **Examples:**
     - A box of assorted chocolates or truffles.
     - Gourmet popcorn, cookies, or biscotti.
     - A selection of premium teas or single-origin coffee beans.

9. **Portable Chargers**
   - **Why They Work:** In our tech-driven world, a portable charger is a lifesaver. It's practical, convenient, and universally useful.
   - **Examples:**
     - Compact power banks for smartphones.
     - Wireless charging pads.
     - Solar-powered portable chargers for eco-conscious recipients.

10. **Board Games or Card Games**

- **Why They Work:** Games encourage social interaction and fun, making them ideal for family gatherings or casual get-togethers.
- **Examples:**
  - Classic games like Scrabble or Uno.
  - Strategy games like Codenames or Ticket to Ride.
  - Portable card games like Exploding Kittens or Sushi Go.

11. **Artisan Soaps or Skincare**

- **Why They Work:** Luxurious soaps and skincare products provide a touch of pampering and are universally appealing.
- **Examples:**

- Handcrafted soaps with natural ingredients.
- Travel-sized skincare kits.
- Moisturizing hand creams in neutral scents.

12. Personalized Gifts

- **Why They Work:** Customization adds a thoughtful touch, making even simple items feel special.
- **Examples:**
    - Monogrammed towels or tote bags.
    - Customized keychains or phone cases.
    - A photo calendar with meaningful pictures.

13. Donation in Their Name

- **Why They Work:** A donation to a cause the recipient cares about is a meaningful way to give back while honoring their values.
- **Examples:**
    - Planting a tree in their name.
    - Donating to a local shelter or charity.
    - Contributing to an organization that supports education, wildlife, or healthcare.

Why These Timeless Choices Never Fail

1. **Universality of Appeal**
   These gifts cater to fundamental human needs—comfort, convenience, and connection—ensuring they resonate across diverse groups.
2. **Practical and Meaningful**
   Practical gifts add value to the recipient's daily life, while meaningful ones foster emotional connections. The gifts on this list strike a balance between the two.
3. **Ease of Customization**
   Many of these gifts can be easily personalized to enhance their emotional impact. A journal can include a heartfelt note, or a plant can come with a decorative pot that reflects the recipient's style.
4. **Low Risk, High Reward**
   These gifts avoid being overly specific, reducing the risk of choosing something the recipient won't use or appreciate. Their versatility ensures they'll be well-received.
5. **Timelessness and Longevity**
   Unlike trendy items, these gifts maintain their appeal over time, making them reliable choices for any occasion.

Conclusion

The Universal Gift List is a collection of timeless, versatile, and thoughtful items that cater to a broad spectrum of tastes and preferences. By choosing from these options, you can ensure your gift will be appreciated and enjoyed, regardless of the recipient's age, background, or interests. Whether it's a soft blanket, a heartfelt donation, or a beautifully designed notebook, these gifts emphasize thoughtfulness and connection, making them perfect for any occasion.

Chapter 11: Gifting Through the Generations

Choosing the perfect gift becomes even more nuanced when you're considering the recipient's age and stage of life. Each generation comes with unique preferences, values, and life experiences that influence what they find meaningful. Understanding these differences is key to selecting gifts that resonate deeply.

This chapter explores how to tailor gifts for different age groups and offers practical advice for cross-generational gifting success. Whether you're shopping for a child, a senior, or someone in between, these tips will help you navigate the complexities of gifting across generations.

How to Choose Gifts That Resonate with Different Age Groups

1. **For Babies and Toddlers (Ages 0–3)**
    - **What They Value:** At this stage, gifts are often chosen more for the parents' convenience or enjoyment than the child's, but items that stimulate development or provide comfort are ideal.
    - **Suggestions:**
        - Soft, cuddly toys like plush animals or sensory blankets.
        - Developmental toys that encourage motor skills, such as stacking blocks or rattles.
        - Personalized keepsakes, like a baby book or a framed photo of the family.
2. **For Young Children (Ages 4–10)**
    - **What They Value:** Young children thrive on play and exploration. Gifts that fuel their creativity and curiosity are perfect.
    - **Suggestions:**

- Interactive toys like LEGO sets, puzzles, or building kits.
- Art supplies, such as crayons, markers, and craft kits.
- Books with engaging stories or characters, tailored to their reading level.

3. **For Tweens (Ages 11–13)**
   - **What They Value:** Tweens are discovering their individuality and interests. Gifts that align with their hobbies or help them express themselves are highly appreciated.
   - **Suggestions:**
     - DIY kits, such as jewelry-making or science experiment sets.
     - Gadgets like wireless earbuds or a smart speaker.
     - Journals or sketchbooks for creative expression.

4. **For Teenagers (Ages 14–19)**
   - **What They Value:** Teens value gifts that reflect their interests, help them stay connected, or enhance their personal style.
   - **Suggestions:**
     - Gift cards to their favorite stores or streaming platforms.
     - Tech accessories, like phone cases, portable chargers, or gaming gear.
     - Trendy clothing or sneakers from brands they love.

5. **For Young Adults (Ages 20–30)**
   - **What They Value:** This group appreciates practical gifts that support their independence, hobbies, or career aspirations.
   - **Suggestions:**
     - Home essentials, such as kitchen gadgets or stylish decor.
     - Subscription services, like meal kits, streaming platforms, or fitness apps.

- Career-oriented gifts, such as a high-quality backpack or professional stationery.

6. **For Middle-Aged Adults (Ages 31–50)**
   - **What They Value:** Middle-aged adults often appreciate gifts that promote self-care, convenience, or family bonding.
   - **Suggestions:**
     - Experience gifts, such as tickets to a concert, theater, or weekend getaway.
     - High-quality cookware or appliances for home chefs.
     - Personalized family mementos, like photo books or custom artwork.

7. **For Seniors (Ages 51 and Older)**
   - **What They Value:** Seniors value gifts that promote comfort, nostalgia, and connection. Practical items and experiences that make their lives easier are also appreciated.
   - **Suggestions:**
     - Memory-evoking gifts, like a scrapbook or a framed family photo.
     - Comfortable items, such as slippers, blankets, or ergonomic pillows.
     - Gadgets designed for simplicity, like a digital photo frame or a user-friendly tablet.

Practical Advice for Cross-Generational Gifting Success

1. **Understand the Recipient's Stage of Life**
   - Consider the life stage they're in. Are they navigating school, building a career, raising a family, or enjoying retirement? Tailor your gift to their current priorities and challenges.
2. **Focus on Shared Experiences**
   - Cross-generational gifts that facilitate connection are particularly meaningful. For example, a family board game can bring people of all ages together, or a cooking class can create shared memories.
3. **Choose Timeless Items**
   - Timeless gifts, like books, high-quality accessories, or handmade crafts, can appeal to recipients across age groups. These items have a universal charm that transcends generational differences.
4. **Incorporate a Personal Touch**
   - A personalized element, such as engraving or tailoring the gift to their preferences, adds a layer of thoughtfulness. This ensures the gift feels meaningful regardless of age.
5. **Consider Practicality and Usability**
   - Gifts that align with the recipient's daily life or solve a specific problem are universally appreciated. For instance, a durable water bottle is as useful to a college student as it is to a senior.
6. **Avoid Generational Stereotypes**
   - Don't assume that all seniors prefer traditional gifts or that all teens want tech gadgets. Focus on the individual's

unique preferences rather than relying on age-based assumptions.

7. **Leverage Technology for Connection**
   - For recipients who live far away, consider digital gifts that bridge the distance, such as e-books, online courses, or virtual experiences.

8. **Combine Sentimentality with Utility**
   - The best cross-generational gifts strike a balance between emotional resonance and practical value. For example, a personalized calendar featuring family photos is both sentimental and functional.

Real-Life Examples of Cross-Generational Gifting

1. **The Multi-Generational Cookbook**
   A family gifted their grandmother a cookbook filled with recipes contributed by each family member. It became a cherished keepsake and encouraged family cooking sessions that bridged the gap between generations.

2. **Board Game Night Starter Kit**
   A thoughtful gift for a family with children, this kit included classic board games, snacks, and a personalized scorecard. It became a tradition that brought all ages together regularly.

3. **The Legacy Journal**
   A grandson gifted his grandfather a journal with prompts about his life experiences and lessons learned. The grandfather not only enjoyed filling it out but also left behind a meaningful legacy for future generations.

4. **Comfort Meets Tech**
   A senior received a digital photo frame preloaded with pictures of their grandchildren. It combined nostalgia with technology, allowing them to feel connected despite the distance.

Why Cross-Generational Gifts Matter

1. **Strengthening Family Bonds**
   Thoughtful gifts can bridge generational gaps, fostering understanding and connection between different age groups.
2. **Encouraging Shared Experiences**
   Gifts that bring people together create opportunities for interaction and relationship-building, regardless of age.
3. **Honoring Life Stages**
   By tailoring gifts to specific life stages, you show empathy and understanding, making the recipient feel seen and valued.
4. **Building a Legacy of Thoughtfulness**
   Cross-generational gifting is an opportunity to pass down traditions, values, and memories, leaving a lasting impression.

Conclusion

Gifting across generations requires a blend of thoughtfulness, practicality, and creativity. By considering the recipient's age, life stage, and preferences, you can choose gifts that resonate deeply and create lasting memories. Whether it's a child's toy that sparks imagination or a senior's keepsake that evokes nostalgia, these gifts have the power to strengthen connections and celebrate the diverse tapestry of life's stages. In the end, the best gifts are those that bring people together, transcending the boundaries of age and time.

Chapter 12: Making Your Gift Legendary

A gift's impact isn't solely determined by what's inside—it's also about how it's presented and delivered. The way you wrap, share, and even tell the story behind your gift can elevate it from a simple gesture to an unforgettable moment. Thoughtful presentation not only enhances the recipient's experience but also deepens the emotional connection they feel to the gift and to you.

This chapter explores the elements of creating a legendary gift-giving experience, from wrapping to timing to the storytelling that can make your gift truly unforgettable.

How to Present and Deliver a Gift to Create Maximum Impact

1. Tailor the Presentation to the Recipient

The first step to legendary gifting is tailoring the presentation to the recipient's personality and preferences. Think about what would delight them the most:

- **Minimalists** appreciate clean, simple packaging with subtle touches, like a ribbon or a handwritten tag.
- **Extravagant types** might love bold, colorful wrapping with elaborate bows or decorations.
- **Sentimental individuals** cherish gifts accompanied by personal notes, photographs, or other meaningful additions.

2. Create a Sense of Anticipation

Building suspense and anticipation can make the moment of opening the gift even more exciting. Consider adding small clues, wrapping the gift in multiple layers, or creating a treasure hunt with the gift as the final reward.

- **Example:** For a travel lover, create a scavenger hunt with travel-themed clues leading to the gift, such as plane tickets or a travel journal.

3. Personalize the Delivery

How you deliver the gift can amplify its emotional impact:

- Hand-deliver it for a personal touch, especially for meaningful gifts.
- Send it through a surprise delivery service for added excitement, like flowers accompanying the gift or a courier dressed as a character the recipient loves.

4. Make the Unwrapping an Experience

The act of unwrapping should feel as special as the gift itself. This can be achieved with creative or interactive wrapping techniques:

- Use reusable materials like fabric wraps, wooden boxes, or decorative tins.
- Hide smaller gifts within larger packages, creating layers of surprise.
- Add an element of fun, like a riddle or puzzle that needs to be solved to access the gift.

5. Timing Is Everything

When you give a gift can make a world of difference:

- **Unexpected moments:** A gift delivered "just because" carries an element of surprise that heightens its emotional impact.
- **Significant milestones:** Timing a gift to coincide with a personal achievement or emotional moment adds depth to the gesture.

The Art of Wrapping, Timing, and Storytelling

1. The Art of Wrapping

Gift wrapping is your first opportunity to make an impression. It sets the tone and builds anticipation for what's inside.

Creative Wrapping Ideas:

- **Themed Wrapping:** Match the wrapping to the gift's theme. For example, wrap a cookbook in a dish towel or a spa set in a soft bathrobe.
- **Eco-Friendly Wrapping:** Use reusable materials like fabric (furoshiki), mason jars, or biodegradable paper to add a sustainable touch.
- **Decorative Touches:** Enhance the wrapping with embellishments like dried flowers, custom tags, or wax seals.

Layering for Intrigue:

- Hide smaller items in progressively larger boxes to create a layered unwrapping experience.
- Incorporate unique containers, like a treasure chest for jewelry or a picnic basket for food-related gifts.

2. The Importance of Timing

The right timing can magnify a gift's emotional impact:

Surprises vs. Expected Gifting:

- **Surprise Moments:** Deliver the gift during an ordinary day to maximize its emotional resonance.
- **Expected Occasions:** Even for expected events like birthdays or holidays, consider giving the gift at a surprising moment during the day, such as first thing in the morning or at a special dinner.

Building Anticipation:

- Use a countdown to the gift-giving moment, such as a daily note, small teaser gifts, or cryptic hints.
- For big reveals, choose a setting that feels significant to the recipient, such as their favorite restaurant or a meaningful location.

3. Storytelling with Your Gift

A story can turn a thoughtful gift into an unforgettable one. Sharing the "why" behind your gift adds layers of meaning and creates a deeper connection.

Crafting a Story:

- Explain what inspired the gift: "I saw this, and it reminded me of the time we…"
- Relate it to a shared memory or milestone: "This is to celebrate how far you've come since…"
- Highlight the symbolism: "This charm represents strength, and I thought it was perfect for you."

Creative Storytelling Techniques:

- **Write a Letter or Note:** Accompany the gift with a heartfelt explanation of its significance.
- **Verbal Delivery:** Share the story aloud when presenting the gift, making eye contact and speaking from the heart.
- **Themed Packaging:** Use the wrapping or box to hint at the story, such as including photos or drawings that relate to the memory.

Examples of Legendary Gift Presentations
1. The Multi-Layered Experience
For a milestone birthday, wrap the gift in several layers, with a small note attached to each layer describing a cherished memory, an inside joke, or a heartfelt message.

2. The Grand Reveal
For a proposal or major life event, hide the gift in an unexpected place. For instance, place a piece of jewelry in a bouquet of flowers or a handwritten note in a book they love, leading to the actual gift.

3. The Story-Inspired Delivery
If you're gifting a photo album, present it during a quiet evening with the recipient and go through the pictures together, recounting the stories behind each one.

4. The Interactive Gift
Turn the gift-giving into an interactive event. For example, if giving tickets to a play, create a custom "invitation" to the event, delivered in a theater-themed package.

Practical Tips for Maximum Impact

1. **Know Your Audience**

   Tailor the presentation style to the recipient. An understated, elegant approach may work for one person, while a bold, over-the-top reveal may resonate with someone else.

2. **Set the Mood**

   Choose the right setting and atmosphere for the gift presentation. Dim lighting, music, or even a themed setup can enhance the experience.

3. **Practice Genuine Delivery**

   Let your emotions shine through. A heartfelt explanation of the gift's significance can make even a simple present feel extraordinary.

4. **Include a Personal Touch**
   Personal elements, such as custom tags, handwritten notes, or inside jokes, make the gift more meaningful.
5. **Embrace Creativity**
   Don't be afraid to think outside the box—literally. Unique containers, wrapping methods, and delivery techniques make the experience unforgettable.

Conclusion

Making your gift legendary isn't just about the item itself—it's about how it's presented, the timing of its delivery, and the story that surrounds it. By putting thought into these elements, you can create an experience that resonates far beyond the act of opening the gift. Whether it's through heartfelt storytelling, creative wrapping, or perfectly timed delivery, a legendary gift leaves a lasting impression that the recipient will cherish for years to come.

Conclusion: The Legacy of Gifting

Gift-giving is far more than an exchange of objects—it's a profound act of connection, love, and thoughtfulness that has the potential to leave a lasting impression. When done with care and intention, a gift becomes more than just a tangible item; it becomes a memory, a symbol, and a bridge between two people. Throughout this book, we've explored the many facets of giving—from the art of surprise and the power of personalization to the timeless impact of universal gifts. Now, as we conclude, it's time to reflect on the legacy of gifting and how the right gift can transform relationships and enrich lives.

The Legacy of Gifting: How the Right Gift Can Leave a Lasting Impression

1. Gifts as Emotional Anchors

A thoughtful gift creates an emotional anchor—a tangible reminder of a specific moment, feeling, or relationship. Long after the wrapping paper is discarded, the emotions tied to the gift remain.

- A photo album can capture years of shared memories, preserving moments that might otherwise fade.
- A simple handwritten note can become a cherished keepsake, treasured for the sincerity and love it conveys.

2. Strengthening Relationships

The right gift demonstrates that you truly see and value the recipient. It communicates, "I know who you are, and I care about you." Over time, these gestures strengthen bonds and build trust, creating relationships that are deeper, more authentic, and more meaningful.

3. Creating Ripples of Joy

The impact of a gift often extends beyond the recipient. When someone receives a thoughtful gesture, they're more likely to pass that kindness on, creating a ripple effect of joy and connection. Your gift, no matter how small, can inspire others to give selflessly and foster a culture of generosity.

4. Gifts as Timeless Treasures

Unlike fleeting trends or disposable items, a truly thoughtful gift has timeless value. A well-chosen book, a handcrafted piece of art, or an experiential gift that creates lasting memories can transcend the moment, becoming a treasured part of the recipient's life story.

5. Enriching the Giver

The act of giving is transformative not only for the recipient but also for the giver. When you give with intention and love, you deepen your own sense of purpose and connection to others. Research shows that generosity boosts happiness, strengthens mental well-being, and fosters a sense of fulfillment.

A Call to Action: Transform the Way You Give Forever

1. Make Every Gift Intentional

From this day forward, commit to giving with intention. Move beyond transactional gifts and instead focus on creating moments of meaning and connection. Ask yourself:

- What does this person truly value?
- How can I make them feel seen, loved, or supported?

2. Think Beyond Material Possessions

Remember, some of the most powerful gifts are intangible. Your time, presence, and emotional support can mean more than any object. Prioritize experiences, acts of service, or heartfelt gestures that show genuine care.

3. Embrace Creativity and Storytelling

Infuse your gifts with creativity and narrative. Whether it's the way you wrap the gift, the story behind it, or the moment of delivery, aim to make the experience as meaningful as the gift itself.

4. Practice Generosity Without Expectations

Shift your mindset to giving for the sake of giving. Let go of any expectations of reciprocation or acknowledgment, and focus solely on the joy of bringing happiness to someone else.

5. Spread the Joy of Giving

Inspire others by embodying the spirit of thoughtful giving. Share your ideas, stories, and experiences to encourage those around you to transform their own approach to gifting.

A Final Thought: The Power of Small Gestures

Never underestimate the impact of a small, thoughtful gift. Even the simplest acts of kindness—a handwritten note, a flower picked from your garden, or a sincere compliment—can have a profound effect. These small gestures, rooted in love and thoughtfulness, remind us that gifting isn't about extravagance—it's about connection.

The Future of Your Gifting Journey

As you close this book, take a moment to imagine the joy you can create, the relationships you can strengthen, and the memories you can forge through thoughtful giving. Each gift you give is an opportunity to leave a lasting legacy—a legacy of love, generosity, and human connection.

This is your call to action. Transform the way you give. Make every gift—whether big or small, tangible or intangible—an expression of your care and a testament to the value you place on your relationships. In doing so, you will not only elevate the act of giving but also enrich your own life and the lives of those around you.

Go forth and give, not just with your hands, but with your heart.

Message from the Author:

I hope you enjoyed this book, I love astrology and knew there was not a book such as this out on the shelf. I love metaphysical items as well. Please check out my other books:

-Life of Government Benefits

-My life of Hell

-My life with Hydrocephalus

-Red Sky

-World Domination:Woman's rule

-World Domination:Woman's Rule 2: The War

-Life and Banishment of Apophis: book 1

-The Kidney Friendly Diet

-The Ultimate Hemp Cookbook

-Creating a Dispensary(legally)

-Cleanliness throughout life: the importance of showering from childhood to adulthood.

-Strong Roots: The Risks of Overcoddling children

-Hemp Horoscopes: Cosmic Insights and Earthly Healing

- Celestial Hemp Navigating the Zodiac: Through the Green Cosmos

-Astrological Hemp: Aligning The Stars with Earth's Ancient Herb

-The Astrological Guide to Hemp: Stars, Signs, and Sacred Leaves

-Green Growth: Innovative Marketing Strategies for your Hemp Products and Dispensary

-Cosmic Cannabis

-Astrological Munchies

-Henry The Hemp

-Zodiacal Roots: The Astrological Soul Of Hemp

- **Green Constellations: Intersection of Hemp and Zodiac**

-Hemp in The Houses: An astrological Adventure Through The Cannabis Galaxy

-Galactic Ganja Guide
Heavenly Hemp
Zodiac Leaves
Doctor Who Astrology
Cannastrology
Stellar Satvias and Cosmic Indicas
<u>Celestial Cannabis: A Zodiac Journey</u>
AstroHerbology: The Sky and The Soil: Volume 1
AstroHerbology:Celestial Cannabis:Volume 2
Cosmic Cannabis Cultivation
The Starry Guide to Herbal Harmony: Volume 1
The Starry Guide to Herbal Harmony: Cannabis Universe: Volume 2
Yugioh Astrology: Astrological Guide to Deck, Duels and more
Nightmare Mansion: Echoes of The Abyss
Nightmare Mansion 2: Legacy of Shadows
Nightmare Mansion 3: Shadows of the Forgotten
Nightmare Mansion 4: Echoes of the Damned
The Life and Banishment of Apophis: Book 2
Nightmare Mansion: Halls of Despair
<u>Healing with Herb: Cannabis and Hydrocephalus</u>
<u>Planetary Pot: Aligning with Astrological Herbs: Volume 1</u>
Fast Track to Freedom: 30 Days to Financial Independence Using AI, Assets, and Agile Hustles
<u>Cosmic Hemp Pathways</u>
How to Become Financially Free in 30 Days: 10,000 Paths to Prosperity
Zodiacal Herbage: Astrological Insights: Volume 1
Nightmare Mansion: Whispers in the Walls
The Daleks Invade Atlantis
Henry the hemp and Hydrocephalus

10X The Kidney Friendly Diet
Cannabis Universe: Adult coloring book
Hemp Astrology: The Healing Power of the Stars
Zodiacal Herbage: Astrological Insights: Cannabis Universe: Volume 2
Planetary Pot: Aligning with Astrological Herbs: Cannabis Universes: Volume 2
Doctor Who Meets the Replicators and SG-1: The Ultimate Battle for Survival
Nightmare Mansion: Curse of the Blood Moon
The Celestial Stoner: A Guide to the Zodiac
Cosmic Pleasures: Sex Toy Astrology for Every Sign
Hydrocephalus Astrology: Navigating the Stars and Healing Waters
Lapis and the Mischievous Chocolate Bar

Celestial Positions: Sexual Astrology for Every Sign
Apophis's Shadow Work Journal: : A Journey of Self-Discovery and Healing
Kinky Cosmos: Sexual Kink Astrology for Every Sign
Digital Cosmos: The Astrological Digimon Compendium
Stellar Seeds: The Cosmic Guide to Growing with Astrology
Apophis's Daily Gratitude Journal

Cat Astrology: Feline Mysteries of the Cosmos
The Cosmic Kama Sutra: An Astrological Guide to Sexual Positions
Unleash Your Potential: A Guided Journal Powered by AI Insights
Whispers of the Enchanted Grove

Cosmic Pleasures: An Astrological Guide to Sexual Kinks
369, 12 Manifestation Journal

Whisper of the nocturne journal(blank journal for writing or drawing)

The Boogey Book

Locked In Reflection: A Chastity Journey Through Locktober

Generating Wealth Quickly:

How to Generate $100,000 in 24 Hours

Star Magic: Harness the Power of the Universe

The Flatulence Chronicles: A Fart Journal for Self-Discovery

The Doctor and The Death Moth

Seize the Day: A Personal Seizure Tracking Journal

The Ultimate Boogeyman Safari: A Journey into the Boogie World and Beyond

Whispers of Samhain: 1,000 Spells of Love, Luck, and Lunar Magic: Samhain Spell Book

Apophis's guides:

Witch's Spellbook Crafting Guide for Halloween

Frost & Flame: The Enchanted Yule Grimoire of 1000 Winter Spells

The Ultimate Boogey Goo Guide & Spooky Activities for Halloween Fun

Harmony of the Scales: A Libra's Spellcraft for Balance and Beauty

The Enchanted Advent: 36 Days of Christmas Wonders

Nightmare Mansion: The Labyrinth of Screams

Harvest of Enchantment: 1,000 Spells of Gratitude, Love, and Fortune for Thanksgiving

The Boogey Chronicles: A Journal of Nightly Encounters and Shadowy Secrets

The 12 Days of Financial Freedom: A Step-by-Step Christmas Countdown to Transform Your Finances

Sigil of the Eternal Spiral Blank Journal

A Christmas Feast: Timeless Recipes for Every Meal

Holiday Stress-Free Solutions: A Survival Guide to Thriving During the Festive Season

Yu-Gi-Oh! Holiday Gifting Mastery: The Ultimate Guide for Fans and Newcomers Alike

Holiday Harmony: A Hydrocephalus Survival Guide for the Festive Season

Celestial Craft: The Witch's Almanac for 2025 – A Cosmic Guide to Manifestations, Moons, and Mystical Events

Doctor Who: The Toymaker's Winter Wonderland

Tulsa King Unveiled: A Thrilling Guide to Stallone's Mafia Masterpiece

Pendulum Craft: A Complete Guide to Crafting and Using Personalized Divination Tools

Nightmare Mansion: Santa's Eternal Eve

Starlight Noel: A Cosmic Journey through Christmas Mysteries

The Dark Architect: Unlocking the Blueprint of Existence

Surviving the Embrace: The Ultimate Guide to Encounters with The Hugging Molly

The Enchanted Codex: Secrets of the Craft for Witches, Wiccans, and Pagans

Harvest of Gratitude: A Complete Thanksgiving Guide

Yuletide Essentials: A Complete Guide to an Authentic and Magical Christmas

Celestial Smokes: A Cosmic Guide to Cigars and Astrology

Living in Balance: A Comprehensive Survival Guide to Thriving with Diabetes Insipidus

Cosmic Symbiosis: The Venom Zodiac Chronicles

The Cursed Paw of Ambition

Cosmic Symbiosis: The Astrological Venom Journal

Celestial Wonders Unfold: A Stargazer's Guide to the Cosmos (2024-2029)

The Ultimate Black Friday Prepper's Guide: Mastering Shopping Strategies and Savings

Cosmic Sales: The Astrological Guide to Black Friday Shopping
Legends of the Corn Mother and Other Harvest Myths
Whispers of the Harvest: The Corn Mother's Journal
The Evergreen Spellbook
The Doctor Meets the Boogeyman
The White Witch of Rose Hall's SpellBook
The Gingerbread Golem's Shadow: A Study in Sweet Darkness
The Gingerbread Golem Codex: An Academic Exploration of Sweet Myths
The Gingerbread Golem Grimoire: Sweet Magicks and Spells for the Festive Witch
The Curse of the Gingerbread Golem
10-minute Christmas Crafts for kids
Christmas Crisis Solutions: The Ultimate Last-Minute Survival Guide
Gingerbread Golem Recipes: Holiday Treats with a Magical Twist
The Infinite Key: Unlocking Mystical Secrets of the Ages
Enchanted Yule: A Wiccan and Pagan Guide to a Magical and Memorable Season
Dinosaurs of Power: Unlocking Ancient Magick
Astro-Dinos: The Cosmic Guide to Prehistoric Wisdom
Gallifrey's Yule Logs: A Festive Doctor Who Cookbook
The Dino Grimoire: Secrets of Prehistoric Magick

If you want solar for your home go here: https://www.harborsolar.live/apophisenterprises/

Get Some Tarot cards: https://www.makeplayingcards.com/sell/apophis-occult-shop

Get some shirts: https://www.bonfire.com/store/apophis-shirt-emporium/

Instagrams:
@apophis_enterprises,
@apophisbookemporium,
@apophisscardshop
Twitter: @apophisenterpr1
Tiktok:@apophisenterprise
Youtube: @sg1fan23477, @FiresideRetreatKingdom
Hive: @sg1fan23477
CheeLee: @SG1fan23477

Podcast: Apophis Chat Zone: https://open.spotify.com/show/5zXbrCLEV2xzCp8ybrfHsk?si=fb4d4fdbdce44dec

Newsletter: https://apophiss-newsletter-27c897.beehiiv.com/

www.ingramcontent.com/pod-product-compliance
Ingram Content Group UK Ltd.
Pitfield, Milton Keynes, MK11 3LW, UK
UKHW032335131224
452403UK00011B/816